The Ripley Scroll

A Facsimile of the Pursuit for the Philosopher's Stone

Victor Shaw

Erebus Society

First published in Great Britain in 2017
Erebus Society

First Edition

Copyright of Text and Arrangement © Victor Shaw 2018
Cover & illustration copyright © Constantin Vaughn 2018

ISBN: 978-1-912461-05-9

www.erebussociety.com

Table of Contents

Introduction

The Ripley

T he 'Ripley scroll' or 'Ripley Scrowle' is a paramount alchemical work of the 15th century as it depicts the mystical and laborious process for the pursuit of the Philosopher's Stone. A legendary substance that can turn base metals into gold and can also be used in the making of the elixir of life, providing its possessor with prolonged life or even Immortality.

This work is associated with the famous English Alchemist George Ripley, and there are approximately 23 copies of the original scroll in existence. Of these, twenty one copies dating from the early 16th to the mid- 17th century, range in size, colours and some other details, but they are all duplicates and variations of the original 15th century Ripley Scroll. Overall, there are two different forms of symbolisms, with seventeen manuscripts of the original version and four of the variations.

Although the scrolls are named after George Ripley, there is no solid evidence that Ripley himself designed the original scroll. They are given the name 'The Ripley Scrolls' because some of them include poetry associated with the alchemist and also, because the male figure at the bottom of the original Ripley Scroll is believed to be George Ripley.

Scrowle

The scroll is about 18 feet 4 inches(5.5m) long and about 23 inches (57.5cms) wide. It consists of seven large sheets of vellum each about 32 inches(80cms) long except for the last section which is 9 inches(22.5cms) long.

Sir George Ripley

Sir George Ripley was an Augustinian canon of Bridlington in Yorkshire who lived from about 1415 to 1495 and one of England's most famous alchemists . He is best known for his work 'The Compound of Alchymy' which he dedicated to Edward IV in 1471.

There were a lot of fables created around his name, especially ones that included stories of his life, his studies, achievements and even his professed death. The myth around him sparked after he published his work 'Liber Duodecim Portarum' (Twelve Gates leading to the Discovery of the Philosopher's Stone) in 1471.

Ever since, his works have been studied by major personalities, alchemists and scientists of the history, such as Dr. John Dee, Robert Boyle, Isaac Newton and more.

On the left: George Ripley, as illustrated in a 16th-century edition of the Ripley Scroll

The
Complete Scroll

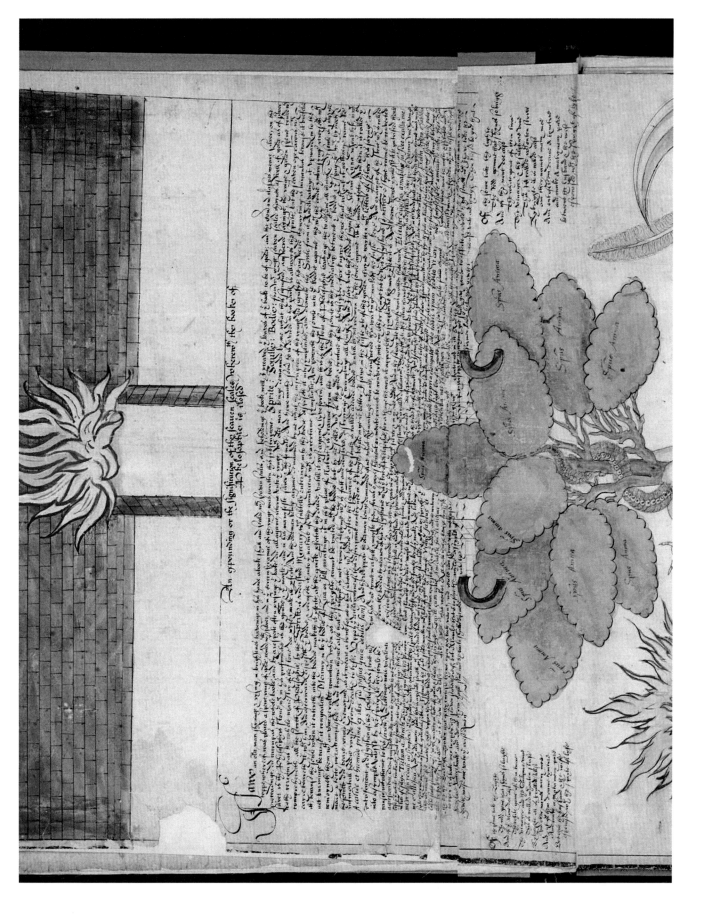

Here is the Sonne whiche is called the mouthe of the collericke

HERE · IS · TE · LAST · OF · Y · RED · AND · Y · BEGINING · TO · PVT · AWAYE · Y · DED · Y · ELEXER · VITE ·

Y MOUTH · OF · Y · COLRICK

Bi boure and hereof   Be voyse

Now understand me what I meane
and take good hede thereto
thy worke else shall litle be done
and come thee to myselfe now
As I have sayde in this fore
Many a name I wryte in bathe
Some behinde and some before
As I schewe there him grewe

He is the mever of all lighte
This Phebus hathe full many a name
He is full harde for to knowe
And if thou knowe not y very same
the whilst thou hast same thou shalt not knowe
therefore if counsell or thou begynne
knowe thine welf what thou be

Hit god shapede y husbande
And Magnetia is his dame
you shall wyslie understand
Nowe I shall here begynne
for to teache thee a ready way
Orelles shall thou some repynt
take good hede what thou seye

In all places where euer so be
he is firste to all liveing thinge
Magnetryner of lyfe to mayke into
And manifeste nature for to springe
bothe the roote benye forthe
for he is a salue in every sore
to brynge about this precious worke

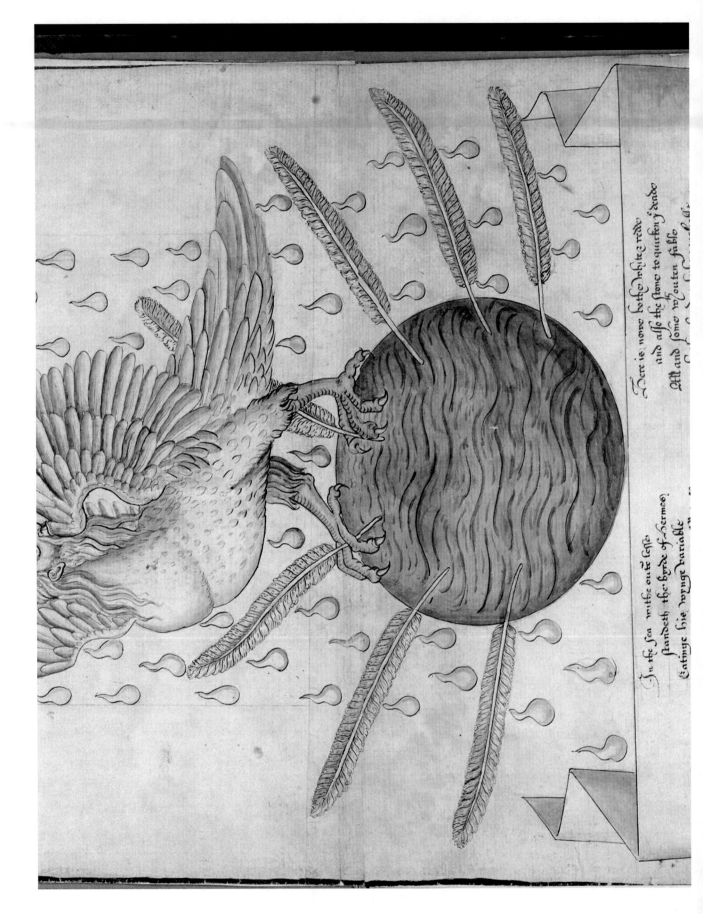

Her is nowe bothe whity z redo
and alfo the stone to quicken y dede
And fome woute fable

In the fea withe oute leffe
ftandeth the byrde of Hermes
eatinge his wynge variable

THE·BEDE·OF·HERMES·IS·MI·NAME·ETING·MI·WINES·TO·MAKE·ME·TAME

THE·RED·SEE·THE·RED·SOL·THE·RED·ELIXER·VITE

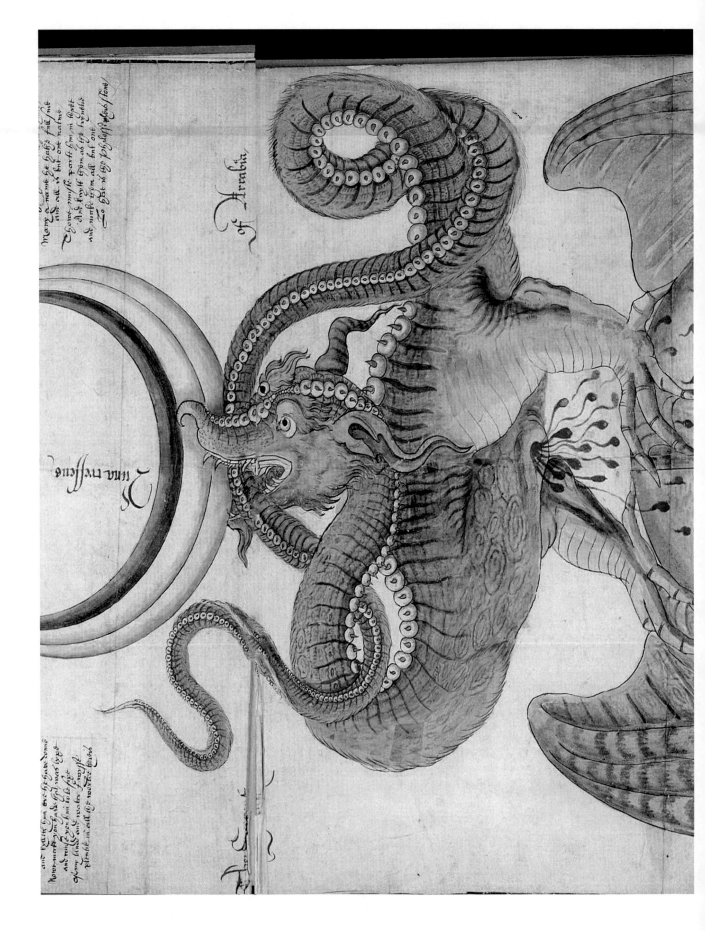

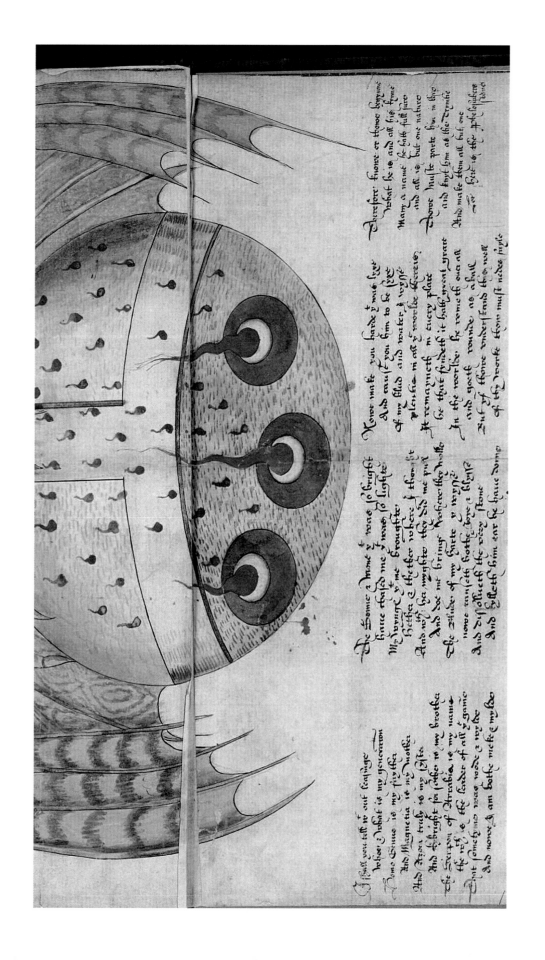

Shall you tell ye out learne
whose I [...] what is my generacion
Some tyme is my fyrthe
And iron truly is my moffer
And Magnetia is my [...]
And bright for softe is my [...]
The serpen of Arrabia is my name
the w[...] the leader of all y game
But sometyme was vade is my [...]
And more I am both [...] my so

The some a name y was so bright
þerre stafed me y was so lighte
My daynar y me broughter
Bettha & thether where y thought
And w[...] þa mayghte þey did me put
And doe me bring þohercther moder
The Aluder of my þarte y myghf
nowe cowpeth þothe þow a blynd
And þiffoluech the very þone
And effecfeth þim oer þe þaue done

Xour make you harde y was þer
And cawfe you þim to be fere
Of my flud and water y wyñe
plenfe in oth y morke fere we
It remayneth in every place
be that findeth it both greatt grace
In the morthe þe remeth ow all
and gooth rounde as a ball
But of þhore vnderftand the well
of thy worke þom muft nede imple

þerefore þhone er þhone bequine
whaf þe is and all his fyme
Many a name þe haf full fure
and all is but one nature
þhone mufte þarte þim in tho
and þhyf þim of the þernthe
And make þem all but one
or fire is the þhelfhhere þone

Deciphering
The Scroll

You must make Water of the Earth, and Earth of the Air, and Air of the Fire,
and Fire of the Earth.
The Black Sea.
The Black Luna.
The Black Sol.
Here is the last of the White Stone and the beginning of the Red.

Of the son take the light
The Red gum that is so bright
And of the Moon do also
The which gum they both trowe
The philosophers Sulphur vive
This I call it without strife
Kybright and Kebright it is called also
And other names many more
Of them drawe out a tincture
And make of them a marriage pure
Between the husband and the wife
Espowsed with the water of life
But of this water thou must beware
Or else thy work will be full bare
He must be made of his own kind
Mark thou now in thy mind
Acetome of philosophers men call this
A water abiding so it is
The maidens milk of the dew
That all the work doth renew
The Serpent of life it is called also
And other names many more

The which causeth generation
Betwixt the man and the woman
But looke thou no division
Be there in the conjunction
Of the moon and of sun
After the marriage be begun
And all the while they be a wedding
Give to them their drinking
Acetome that is good and fine
Better to them then any wine
Now when this marriage is done
Philosophers call it a stone
The which hath a great nature
To bring a stone that is so pure
So he have kindly nourishment
Perfect heat and decoction
But in the matrix when they be put
Let never the glasse be unshut
Till they have ingendred a stone
In the world there not such a one

The Red Lune. The Spirit of Water. Red Sol. The Red Sea.

On the ground there is a hill
Also a serpent within a well
His tail is long with wings wide
All ready to flee by every side
Repair the well fast about
That thy serpent pass not out
For if that he be there a gone
Thou lose the virtue of the stone
Where is the ground you must know here
And the well that is so clear
And what is the dragon with the tail
Or else the work shall little avail
The well must run in water clear
Take good heed for this your fire
The fire with water bright shall be burnt
And water with fire washed shall be
The earth on fire shall be put
And water with air shall be knit
Thus ye shall go to purification
And bring the serpent to redemption
First he shall be black as a crow
And down in his den shall lie full low

Swelling as a toad that lieth on the ground
Burst with bladders sitting so round
They shall to burst and lie full plain
And this with craft the serpent is slain
He shall shine colors here many a one
And turn as white as whale's bone
With the water that he was in
Wash him clear from his sin
And let him drink a little and a light
And that shall make him fair and white
The which whiteness be abiding
Lo here is a very full finishing
Of the white stone and the red
Lo here is the very true deed.

Ye MOVTH OF Ye COLRICKE

HERE·IS·Ye·LAST·OF·Ye·RED·AND·Ye·BEGINING·TO·PVT·AWAYE·Ye·DED·Ye·ELEXER·VITE

The Red Lion.
The Green Lion.
The Mouth of Choleric beware.
Here is the last of the Red, and the beginning to put away the dead.
The Elixir Vitae.

Take the father that
Phoebus so high
That sit so high in majesty
With his beams that shines so bright
In all places wherever that he be
For he is father to all things
Maintainer of life to crop and root
And causeth nature for to spring
With the wife beginneth soothe
For he is salve to every sore
To bring about this prosperous work
Take good heed unto this lore
I say unto learned and unto clerk
And Homogenie is my name
Which God made with his own hand
And Magnesia is my dame
You shall verily understand.
Now I shall here begin
For to teach thee a ready way
Or else little shall thou win
Take good heed what I do say
Divide thou Phoebus in many parts
With his beams that be so bright
And this with nature him convert
The which is mirror of all light
This Phoebus hath full many a name
Which that is full hard to know
And but thou take the very same

The philosophers stone ye shall not know
Therefore I counsel ere ye begin
Know it well what it should be
And that is thick make it thin
For then it shall full well like thee
Now understand what I mean
And take good heed thereto
Our work else shall little be seen
And turn thee to much woe
As I have said this our lore
Many a name I wish he hath
Some behind and some before
As philosophers doth him give
In the sea without lees
Standeth the bird of Hermes
Eating his wings variable
And maketh himself yet full stable
When all his feathers be from him gone
He standeth still here as a stone
Here is now both white and red
And all so the stone to quicken the dead
All and some without fable
Both hard and soft and malleable
Understand now well and right
And thank you God of this sight

THE·RED·SEE·THE·RED·SOL·THE·RED·ELIXER·VITE

The bird of Hermes is my name
Eating my wings to make me tame.
The Red Sea.
The Red Sol.
The Red Elixir Vitae.
Red Stone.
White Stone.
Elixir Vitae.
Luna in Crescent.

I shall you tell with plain declaration
Where, how, and what is my generation
Omogeni is my Father
And Magnesia is my Mother
And Azot truly is my Sister
And Kibrick forsooth is my Brother
The Serpent of Arabia is my name
The which is leader of all this game
That sometime was both wood and wild
And now I am both meek and mild
The Sun and the Moon with their might
Have chastised me that was so light
My wings that me brought
Hither and thither where I thought
Now with their might they down me pull,
And bring me where they will
The Blood of mine heart I wish
Now causeth both joy and blisse
And dissolveth the very Stone
And knitteth him ere he have done

Now maketh hard that was lix
And causeth him to be fix
Of my blood and water I wish
Plenty in all the World there is
It runneth in every place
Who it findeth he hath grace In the
World it runneth over all
And goeth round as a ball
But thou understand well this
Of the worke thou shalt miss
Therefore know ere thou begin
What he is and all his kin
Many a name he hath full sure
And all is but one Nature
Thou must part him in three
And then knit him as the Trinity
And make them all but one
Lo here is the Philosophers Stone